INNOVATIVE APPROACHES TO TEACH COMMUNICATION SKILLS

DR. T. S. SANTHI

Copyright © Dr. T. S. Santhi
All Rights Reserved.

TO EVERY LANGUAGE LEARNER

Contents

Contents

Foreword

One of the commonly discussed topics about the psychology of students is about retaining their focus on subjects for a longer period. Psychologists widely agree that while the attention span of individuals may vary from a minimum of 8 seconds to a maximum of 40 minutes, they also agree that this variation depends on the task on hand. The attention span also depends on various physical and psychological factors of the individual like interest to do the task, congenial environment, well-equipped workplace, knowledge sustenance, and so on. Considering all the factors, it is well understood that a heterogeneous group of learners will pose a big challenge to a teacher. The teacher will have to study the overall mindset of the learners, identify common or major interests shared and design teaching strategies accordingly. Implementing the designed strategies play a vital role. Any learning material which does not hold the attention of the learners for the expected span of time has to be eliminated immediately and should be replaced with a fresh one. Hence the process of teaching English as a second language requires a lot of creativity so that it caters to the needs of 21st-century learners.

Acknowledgements

My sincere thanks to the College Management for their support and encouragement. The management has always supported me in all the endeavors. It is because of their · constant encouragement I am able to take bolder steps.

Thanks to the team of content editors who worked very hard to bring my thoughts to words.

My love and affection to my friends who stood by me and encouraged me to go with this long-pending idea.

Gratitude to the Almighty for taking me to the right people at the right time to bring this book out.

CHAPTER ONE

INTRODUCTION

ATTENTION RETENTION IN STUDENTS

Retention of students' interest and attention, the biggest challenge faced by all teachers, especially those who teach English as a second language, is one that requires a lot of effort and dedication from the teacher's side. A movie which plays for about three hours includes song sequences, stunts, suspense factors, comic factors and so on to keep the audience glued to their seats. Those movie makers who study the shifts in the audience's mood and cater to the needs perfectly relish success; those who falter fail. If a concept of entertainment which demands more from the makers involves so many factors, it is not a wonder that the concept of teaching English as a second language demands much more. Learners of English as a second language face too many difficulties initially, and every difficulty is blown to a mega size just because of the fear of learning a new language is created within. The learners' minds carry the following thoughts:

- "Will I be able to speak in English as the others do?"
- "Will others laugh at my mistakes?"
- "What will others think if I do not grasp the language quickly?"
- "Will I understand the concepts and put them into proper use?"
- "Will the teacher help me understand the nuances of language?"
- "Will the teacher help me patiently?"

There are always counter thoughts from the teacher's side.

- "How will the mixed group of learners respond to the learning materials?"
- "Will the concepts and illustrations be understood?"
- "Will the learners be receptive?"
- "Will the materials be interesting enough to hold their attention for a longer time?"

With so many thoughts and doubts swarming about in their minds, teachers and learners strive hard to impress each other and to derive maximum output. Considering these factors, we can understand that the needs of the teachers and learners complement one another, thereby leading to a very effective teaching-learning process. While the teachers want the learners to be receptive, participative and assertive, the learners want the teachers to be innovative, patient and motivating. The needs of both the sides can be satisfied provided the methods adopted by the teachers of ESL are thought out of the box.

• 3 •

CHAPTER TWO

WHAT DO LEARNERS EXPECT FROM LANGUAGE TEACHERS?

A live experiment showed that the learners have the following expectations towards their language teachers.

- The learners want the teachers to tune their minds to that of students' frequency

- They want more activities rather than mere theories or illustrations
- They want the teachers to cater to all their needs equally and not be biased
- They require an assertive teacher who also participates instead of being a mere audience

Summing up these expectations, several methods of teaching were carried out to two different sets of ESL learners. One set of learners constituted of students with sufficient knowledge of the basics of grammar and sentence patterns of English but with limited scope for speaking in various scenarios. The other set of learners constituted students who had minimal exposure to not only grammar and sentence patterns but also lacked awareness of the majority of words in English. The teaching process was carried out in 8 stages.

1. Initial teaching of the basic concepts to both sets of learners
2. Splitting them to give different activities to work on the concept taught
3. Explaining separately the details necessary for the groups to perform better
4. Discussing the outcomes of the activities common to both sets of learners
5. Giving the learners a few illustrations that will commonly be understood
6. Providing them with similar exercises to work upon
7. Analysing the results and discussing the same to help them correct their mistakes
8. Testing them with the help of an unbiased question paper

Of these, stages 2, 5 and 6 were eagerly received by the learners, as a result of which stage 8 (testing) was not dreaded.

5 Stages of
SECOND LANGUAGE ACQUISITION

SILENT OR RECEPTIVE PHASE

In this first stage, second language learners dedicate time to learning vocabulary of the new language. They may also practice saying new terms.

EARLY PRODUCTION

This second phase involves the second language user beginning to "collect" new words. During this time they may also start to say some terms and may even begin forming short phrases of early word combinations.

SPEECH EMERGENCE OR PRODUCTION

By the time second language learners enter into this third stage, they have collected several thousand words.
This is an exciting phase as they begin to communicate by combining these learned words into short phrases and sentences - their second language is truly becoming "connected".

INTERMEDIATE FLUENCY

The fourth level is said to occur when speakers begin communicating in complex sentences (that is, sentences will include conjunctions to sequence and connect related clauses).

This is a critical stage for allowing even more connected language and true conversations to emerge. Second language learners may also begin to think in their second language at this time, again reflecting the significant progress that has been made.

CONTINUED LANGUAGE DEVELOPMENT OR FLUENCY

This stage may last for an extended time. Here, second language learners will continue to develop their new language and to achieve accuracy with increasing complexity and with social pragmatics.

CHAPTER THREE

ACTIVITIES TO TRY IN YOUR CLASS

The following are few of the activities that were carried out in the classroom for the benefit of ESL learners.

Activity 1: Who am I?

A volunteer from the learners is sent outside while the rest of the class thinks of a famous person whose name the volunteer should guess by asking questions. The rule to be remembered by the volunteer is that the rest of the class would answer only "Yes/NO" and thus he/she should ask question in such a way that the answer helps in identifying the person. For example: If the person is Dr. A P J Abdul Kalam, the volunteer can begin the questioning session like "Is the person a male?", "Is he an Indian?", "Does he hold any important position?", "Was he the President?" and so on. The number of questions can be limited to 10 or 20 so that he/she gets to guess sooner. This activity helps the learners frame questions with the help of modals and auxiliaries, and this involves the entire set of learners to participate hence eradicating the differences among their capacities.

Activity 2: Yesterday; Today; Tomorrow

This is one of the simplest methods to teach ESL learners the tenses. The teacher can ask the students to list out a few of their daily actions, give various tense forms for a few important verbs in English, and make them use the actions in sentences to denote various tenses. For example: if the list includes something like **brushing teeth, taking bath, going to college, studying;** the teacher should ask, "What did you do yesterday?"; and the learners would answer, "I brushed my teeth, took bath, went to college and studied." This can be carried out to other tenses as well.

Activity 3: What did he/she say?

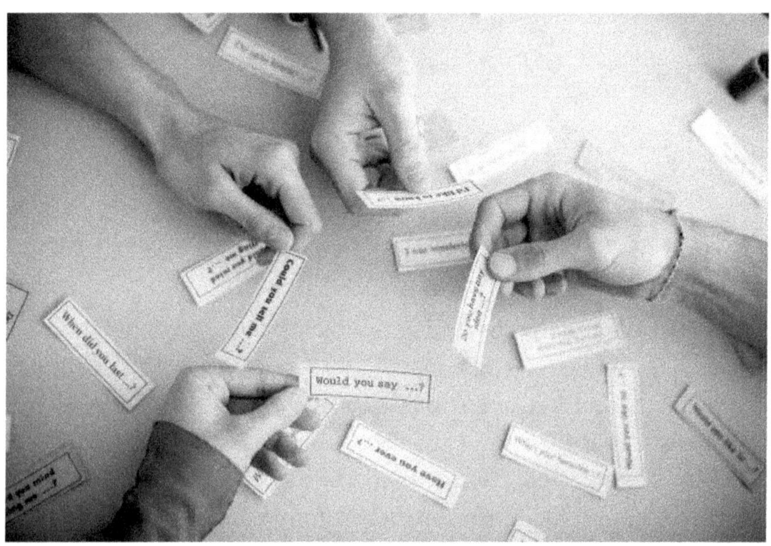

This activity needs the learners to work in pairs. The students in each pair would ask a few basic questions to know about each other and would take down the answers. Once the answers are taken down, the teacher would put the question, "What did he/she say?" Each of the learners would then interpret their partner's answers and provide them in reported speech. For example: "She is XYZ. She said that she like listening to melodious songs. She told me she likes science fiction..."

Activity 4: Describe me

The teacher will have to collect lot of pictures which depict commonly used or known objects. The pictures are to be displayed for about a minute or two after which they are hidden from the class. Then the learners are supposed to list out all the objects they found in the pictures describing each of them in single word. For example: if the picture showed a dog playing with a ball, the learner can say "The **naughty** dog is playing with a **big** ball." This helps the learners know about a huge list of adjectives.

Activity 5: Act 'em out

DUMB CHARADES

The teacher has to write idioms and phrases on small chits of paper. Each student gets a chance to pick from the lot and to act out the idioms or phrases they get. When the rest guess correctly the teacher gets to explain the same and give few sentences to explain the usage. The same can be done to know synonyms and antonyms of words as well.

Activity 6: Once upon a time...

This is one chance to let the learners let their imagination take wings. The teacher can encourage the students to put all that they have learnt to frame stories of their own. The learners can seek help when they face difficulties with sentence formation or word usage. The most advanced level would involve writing poems where the students can be encouraged to use a thesaurus to use peculiar words equivalent to those common ones.

Teachers of ESL have a huge canvas to paint on. It is purely one's own creativity and interest that would pave way to lot more activities to keep young learners engaged for a desired period. The more the teachers create, the more the learners tend to get themselves involved actively in the learning process. It is so much like coating pills with sugar to make it taste better.

CHAPTER FOUR

HOW DO NEOPHYTES LEARN?

Learning is an experience which takes an individual a step ahead in terms of knowledge and wisdom. The experience may vary from individual to individual. As the biological age increases in an individual, the ability to learn also increases. This increase might be in terms of quality or quantity, and purely depends on the person. While an individual might learn a particular concept to increase his or her knowledge in a particular field, another might learn the same to make a living out of it, and yet another might learn the same to pursue a different goal. Thus the reasons for learning differ too. Thus emerge varieties of styles in learning. These varieties can be studied straightforwardly by observing young learners or beginners in any field. They can be called neophytes who have different styles of learning. These neophytes range from school-going children to those who are employed immediately after a degree. This paper is an attempt to converge various learning theories that deal with different learning styles that can be understood better with live illustrations and real learning scenarios. In short, this is an endeavor to study how neophytes learn.

CHAPTER FIVE

THE PROCESS OF LANGUAGE LEARNING & TEACHING

The process of learning a language begins as soon as a child is brought into this world. It hears different sounds not comprehending the meanings or differences between each of them. As its sensory organs develop, the child starts differentiating sounds and slowly starts imitating them as well. The words that it frequently hears, being uttered by its parents and other members of the family, are grasped and thus it starts learning the language of the house. Once it advances from imitating the words and sounds of the language to producing words in response to those it's spoken to, the child is then introduced to reading those words in fonts. Only at a later stage the child starts writing the words of the language. Thus the four steps involved in the process of language learning – LSRW (Listening, Speaking, Reading and Writing) – leads the child to learn the language effectively.

LSRW has been acknowledged as the most effective strategy for learning a language. Sadly, this is not followed in many schools that teach students English as a second language. Indian children in schools are the most complicated heterogeneous learning group to be tackled by an English teacher since they always are from varied language backgrounds and cultures. "The 2001 census mentioned

122 Indian languages . . ." (Ganesh N Devy). With over 100 languages, teaching a target language is indeed difficult. But the difficulties could easily be overcome if the LSRW pattern is followed. But what happens in most of the Indian schools is that the teachers introduce the alphabet first, make the students memorize a few words, and make them write simultaneously, thus totally eliminating the need for teaching them how to speak and read the language. Listening becomes an invisible component, and only writing predominates. Even this becomes a burden to the students when they are pushed towards a target in the name of results and grades. Instead of influencing the students to learn the new language, the teachers terrorize them. Thus, very few grasp the language part, and the majority only view the entire process as yet another subject. This not only demotivates the beginners but also curbs any new ones from learning the language as well.

So, how can a teacher create a conducive atmosphere for neophytes learning a new language? According to an article titled The Principles of Teaching and Learning published by The Department of Education and Childhood Development (2002), students learn best when:

- the learning environment is supportive and productive;
- the learning environment promotes independence, cooperation and self-motivation;
- their needs, backgrounds, perspectives and interests are reflected in the program;
- they are challenged and supported to develop and apply their thinking;
- their learning progress is monitored; and
- their learning reflects the way things are currently done in the community

CHAPTER SIX

RENOVATION OF LANGUAGE AT THE KEYS OF COMPUTERS

Ever since mankind's evolution began, communication topped man's list of needs. He needed to communicate with his fellow beings to convey and receive messages. Communication enabled him to socialize with his fellow beings. It allowed him to share, learn and most of all, to live. Thus it was after man started communicating he became a true social being. Communication does not mean that man started conversing using any proper language. At first I was mere signs, gestures, sounds, facial expressions and crude drawings. Over a period of time, man understood that the crude sounds he used could be modified into various ways by either raising or lowering the noise levels. He even tried imitating the sounds of animals, trees and birds. This added on to his vociferous vocabulary. Man slowly started modifying the basic sounds and thus evolution of language began.

Many scientists believe that language originated much before the ability of speech evolved. The pre-historic man's 'monkey call', 'leopard call', 'snake call' and so on may be called the first of the languages that evolved. While language is much easier task, the ability of speech is more complicated and difficult to acquire. This is because language is formed by combining several sounds to form words and sentences; whereas speech involves combination of vocal chords, speech organs and respiratory organs. In short, reception of sounds is easier than production of the same sounds. With sounds modified to communicate vocally, languages came into existence. Man used his languages to communicate among people who understood the same. From oral production of sounds, man induced those into writing and thus alphabet, words, sentence formats were evolved. Today, apart from oral language and written language, we have a new branch of literature e-language or the language of the computers. Though the only language the computers and other electronic gadgets could understand is the binary language which consists of 'one's and 'zero's, these binary units actually are used to interpret human languages that are fed into them. Thus an internal translation takes place and human languages are understood by the machines. Today, computers can understand and interpret almost all the languages in the world.

Every language underwent and still undergoes lot of changes or phases of transformation ever since they evolved. One among such languages is 'the window on the world', 'language of the commons', 'the third most natively spoken language in the world', English. English is a West Germanic language that arose in the Anglo-Saxon kingdoms of England. It is widely learned as a second language and used as an official language of the European Union and many Commonwealth countries, as well as in many world organizations. Modern English is the direct descendant of Middle English, itself a direct descendant of Old English, a descendant of Proto-Germanic. Thus the various phases of the transformation of English can be traced from the Proto-Germanic which is the unattested ancestor that is said to have evolved around 750 BC, Old English or the Anglo-Saxon which is said to have evolved around mid 5th century, Middle English which is said to have evolved around 13th century and Modern English which began its evolution around 16th century. Though English has undergone several changes over so many centuries through the pens of several literary geniuses and language experts and the people themselves, ever since the advent of computers it has gone through a new phase of change. English has taken a totally new syntax, morphology and usage. We can even name the phase e-English or Electronic English.

With all these various alterations in English language, the modernized version is the simplest of all. Yet computers have offered to simplify the simplified version of English. With several new advancements in the field of computer technology like the e-mails, chats, texts and so on, English has been greatly simplified to what we can e-English or Electronic English. New abbreviations have been introduced to save time and increase efficiency of communication. Few examples can be quoted:

K – ok, TC – Take Care, BFF – Best Friends Forever, 2 – to, LOL – Laugh Out Loud, ASAP – As Soon As Possible, Gr8 – Great, TX – Thanks, Plz – Please, IC – I See, GM – Good Morning.

Thus English has almost been abbreviated to suit the needs and time of the users. This change, unlike the changes that English underwent few centuries back, cannot be called beneficial. While the previous changes were done to simplify the language, this modern change is just to make the language look more flashy and undemanding. Computer users all over the world find the e-English very viable. But the sad truth is that e-English has been distributed rapidly among the young minds of the world, thus luring them to use the same in academic scenarios too. While computers help one greatly in all that one does, it can be a great hindrance to one's creativity and thought flow. It only thwarts the healthy development of the language. Today youngsters are adhered to the screens of their mobiles and computers. Texting, chatting and mailing have outdated face-to-face conversations, letters and get-togethers. Loss of interest in books has taken the younger generation even farther away from a flair for English as a language. Not even e-books have any impact on them. It only signifies that English is undergoing a very drastic phase of transformation which will result in English becoming a coded language.

CHAPTER SEVEN

SLANG OR NOT TO SLANG

Meaning

* British slang is English language slang used and originating in the United Kingdom.
* Slang is the use of informal words and expressions that are not considered standard in the speaker's dialect or language.

Another important factor in e-English is the use of slangs. Slang is the use of informal words and expressions that are not considered standard in the speaker's dialect or language. Few examples for slang: cool, dude, kid, howdy, chill, etc. While addition of words from other languages can be healthy and helpful in the growth of a language, use of unethical words and undemanding expressions can only mar the growth of that language. Few linguists have endeavored to clearly define what constitutes slang. Attempting to remedy this, Bethany K. Dumas and Jonathan Lighter argue that an expression should be considered "true slang" if it meets at least two of the following criteria:

- It lowers, if temporarily, "the dignity of formal or serious speech or writing"; in other words, it is likely to be considered in those contexts a "glaring misuse of register."

- Its use implies that the user is familiar with whatever is referred to, or with a group of people who are familiar with it and use the term.

- "It is a taboo term in ordinary disclosure with people of a higher social status or greater responsibility."

- It replaces "a well-known conventional synonym." This is done primarily to avoid the discomfort caused by the conventional item or further elaboration.

Using slangs has the following disadvantages:

- First, it creates a barrier to communication for the uninitiated.

- Second, because most slang is short and lively, favoring one-syllable words, it leads to the use of clichés, rather than the use of more precise words.

- Dependence on slang can lead to unclear thinking.

On many occasions the use of slangs and abbreviations is even considered highly impolite and sometimes even abusive. Does this mean one cannot use abbreviations or slangs in one's writings or speeches? The answer is, no. One can use abbreviations and slangs in writings and speeches, but one must ensure that those abbreviations and slangs contribute to the growth of the language and not mar the growth. Limiting the use of slangs and abbreviations to specific scenarios is a must in order to keep the language unpolluted. Unpolluted language will help in a healthy transition or transformation as days pass by. What the future needs is a language with proper words and syntax and not a language with mere codes and letters. Renovation of language cannot be left at the mercy of the keys of computers. It is always at the hands of learned people and scholars who can bring a healthy and smooth transition to any language.

THE EXUBERANCE OF TEACHING AND LEARNING ENGLISH

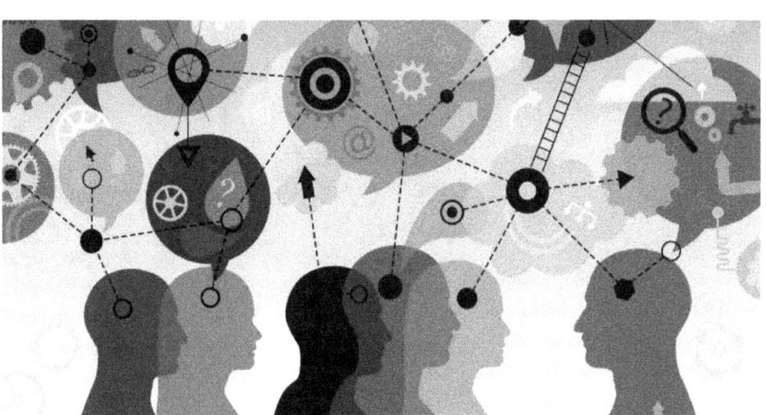

Over the years of study, scientists and researchers have found that concepts taught with a blend of fun have always been grasped at a faster pace by the students and the results were always better too. In order to make learning a fun process teaching ought to be relaxed and exuberant too. Hence the need to innovation and creativity in the process of teaching arises, so as to make learning interesting and effective. Several games and fun activities have been designed by educationists and language experts to enable the teaching-learning process interesting to both the teacher and the taught. But over a period the fun factors have been lost due to several constraints like time, frame of syllabus, necessity to induce external factors, attitude of the students and so on. The current attitude of the students' community is such that they have access to every possible external learning source which leaves them in no special need for a teacher. But the one thing which the modern electronic gadgets cannot supplement is the innovation factor. They do not have the power to retain the students and enable them to completely grasp the necessary concepts. Especially, learning languages is not possible without a human teacher. This paper deals with need for creativity and innovation in the teaching-learning process of languages, especially English. It also illustrates few activities which will make both teaching and learning exuberant.

CHAPTER NINE

STEP-BY-STEP PROCESS OF LEARNING A LANGUAGE

Right from the time a child is born it starts acquiring its mother tongue by listening to the conversations around it. It listens to its mother, father, and other relatives talk to it and among themselves and tries to decipher the sounds spoken. Though the child does not have the cognitive ability then, it slowly develops with its physical growth. Thus the first step in learning a language is "Listening". When it is about a year or two older the child begins to differentiate various speech sounds and also tries to reproduce or imitate or frame sounds of its own. It starts speaking the language spoken by its parents. It steps in to the next phase "Speaking". Once the child starts taking formal education, it enters the next two phases

"Reading" and "Writing".

Every language is learnt best only if the LSRW method is followed. But learning can be tiresome since application closely follows; and incorrect application often leads to ridicule and mockery. Over the years of study, scientists and researchers have found that concepts taught with a blend of fun have always been grasped at a faster pace by the students and the results were always better too. In order to make learning a fun process teaching ought to be relaxed and exuberant too. Hence the need to innovation and creativity in the process of teaching arises, so as to make learning interesting and effective.

Several games and fun activities have been designed by educationists and language experts to enable the teaching-learning process interesting to both the teacher and the taught. But over a period the fun factors have been lost due to several constraints like time, frame of syllabus, necessity to induce external factors, attitude of the students and so on. The current attitude of the students' community is such that they have access to every possible external learning source which leaves them in no special need for a teacher. But the one thing which the modern electronic gadgets cannot supplement is the innovation factor. They do not have the power to retain the students and enable them to completely grasp the necessary concepts. Especially, learning languages is not possible without a human teacher. How much ever the electronic gadgets and softwares help in the process of learning languages, it is a human teacher who can actually test the students' level of understanding and correct them when they go wrong. Surveys prove that language learning was effective in the yesteryears when electronic gadgets were never invented. Fact-to-face communication enabled people to grasp any new language. Reading and writing further enhanced their knowledge of the language and thus people learnt several languages. Direct contact with the teacher helped them connote concepts to practical factors and thus the learning process was faster.

CHAPTER TEN

ACTIVITIES FOR TEACHERS TO TRY IN CLASS

Connotation always plays a very important role in the learning process. Especially in the process of learning languages, connotation, which the Oxford Advanced Learner's Dictionary defines as "an idea suggested by a word in addition to its main meaning", plays a vital role. This can be substantiated with the following illustration.

Example: The teacher wants to explain the meaning and usage of the idiom "Pull the plug".

Formal explanation:

"To pull the plug means to stop an event from happening. For example; 'when things started going out of control I had to pull the plug.'"

Connotative explanation:

Teacher: Do you like listening to songs?

Students: Yes!

Teacher: If I bring in a tape recorder and play songs now, will you like it?

Students: Of course, yes!

Teacher: Let us say I pull out the plug all on a sudden. What will happen?

Students: The music would not play. It would stop!

Teacher: If I pull the plug, music would......?

Students: Stop!

Teacher: Good! So, the idiom "To pull the plug" means.....?

Students: To stop something?

Teacher: Yes, you are right! It means to stop something from happening or from proceeding.

In the above illustration, the teacher tries to connote the idiom "to pull the plug" with a real-life situation, thus enabling the students to decipher the meaning by themselves.

Letting the students discover the answers all by themselves not only induces interest in learning but also creates a congenial atmosphere for leaning. It relieves the students off the stress and makes them relish the learning process. There are numerous ways to make learning exciting. But over all it depends on the method that the teacher employs. One of the techniques which will never fail to attract students is play-way method. A mélange of fun with studies will satisfy both the teacher and the taught.

There are several important aspects of learning languages. The most important ones are vocabulary acquisition, sentence formation, grammar and application. These aspects are most often considered too uninteresting and dry. Hence the students dislike the theoretical part of learning a language. It proves a great challenge for the teachers too to break the wall that has erupted and to bring the students back to the learning process. In order to prevent such walls from erupting, the employment of the play-way method can be very effective. This method demands high creativity, innovative techniques and patience. The following methods can be employed in the process of teaching and learning various aspects of a language.

CHAPTER ELEVEN

TEACHING VOCABULARY

Ever individual's vocabulary can be split into active and passive. Active vocabulary consists of a set of words that are often put to use with complete or partial knowledge about the words. Passive vocabulary consists of words that are seldom or never used due to unfamiliarity of meaning and usage. When words in active vocabulary are used sparsely, they tend to get accumulated in the passive vocabulary. Like wise if the words in passive vocabulary are often used and meanings are learnt, they get added to one's active vocabulary. This movement takes place in every individual's mind. In order to reduce the number of words in passive vocabulary and to increase the number in active vocabulary the following games can be employed in classroom teaching.

1. Word Disintegration: This is probably one of the oldest and commonest of all word games. The teacher would give a difficult word and ask the students to derive known words using the letters in the parent word.

Example: "Exuberance" – bar, bear, ear, can, cab, ran, race, etc.

This game not only kindles the active vocabulary of the students but also provokes wider thinking and a flair for the language.

2. Word Scramble: In this game the teacher would jumble the letters in a word and would ask the students to find the word as well as other smaller words hidden.

Example: "L U A R M" – arm, lam, mar, ram, rum, alum, arum, marl, maul, mural

This game not only kindles the active vocabulary but also the passive vocabulary, helping the students to recollect several forgotten words and to familiarize their meanings and usage.

3. Snakes and Ladders: This game has been played for over several generations as a mere pastime. The same can be used to teach vocabulary as well just by adding in a few rules. The board can be set in such a way that every ladder is always accompanied with a snake too. This way whenever a person is about to reach the cell with the ladder and snake, he or she has to answer a question related to vocabulary, either by giving the meaning for a word given or by using the word in a sentence. If the student is able to answer, he or she gets to climb the ladder; else he or she comes down the snake.

4. Dumb Charades: This too is a well-known game. The teacher can split the class into groups and give words to representatives from each group. The representatives would enact to his or her group to spot the correct word. Bonus marks could be given to those who can use the words into sentences and can give the meanings as well.

5. Picture idioms: The teacher could collect a few pictures that can signify an idiom and ask the students to guess the idiom. A few pictures are given below. Each represents an idiom. The meanings of the idioms are also given.

PICTURE IDIOMS

MORE FUN ACTIVITIES FOR COMMUNICATION CLASSES

There are several more games that could be employed in classrooms to teach new words and their meanings. A few other common activities are "match the correct synonyms", "correct the spellings", "dictionary hunt", and so on. These activities also promote the students to use a dictionary. Thus their passive vocabulary shrinks and active vocabulary grows.

CHAPTER TWELVE

TEACHING SENTENCE PATTERNS

Sentence patterns in English are different from that in several other languages. Hence Grammar-Translation method will not help much in the process. Direct method is the most appropriate method using which a teacher can ensure the sentence patterns are deciphered properly. Sentence patterns in English have always been taught in schools using Subject, Verb and Predicate; using abbreviations to symbolize each category and asking students to frame sentences accordingly. However, formation of sentences can be taught better using the following methods.

1. Enact the sentence patterns: In this method, the teacher could call out a few students to represent a subject and an object, make them perform some actions and explain the verb and the relationship between the subject and the object.

Example: A student gives a pen to another student. Teacher can explain that the student A is the Subject, pen is the Direct Object, student B is the Indirect Object and the action of giving is the Verb.

2. Jumble, arrange and shuffle: In this method the teacher can write out nouns and verbs in pieces of papers and jumble them. The students can be split into groups and made to frame sentences in various patterns using the various nouns and verbs. This would help them broaden up their thinking capacity. The papers could be shuffled and reshuffled to frame a huge variety of sentences.

3. Spot in the story: This is one of the most interesting methods which might help students to learn sentence patterns faster. A story can be printed out and circulated among the students. The students can split themselves into groups and identify various sentence patterns in the story. This would enhance their reading skills as well.

Though there are several more play-way methods of teaching, sentence patterns and formation have always been a big challenge for the teachers as well as students due to the influence of mother-tongue. Hence it is advisable to carry out teaching sentence formations at a later stage in the process of teaching languages.

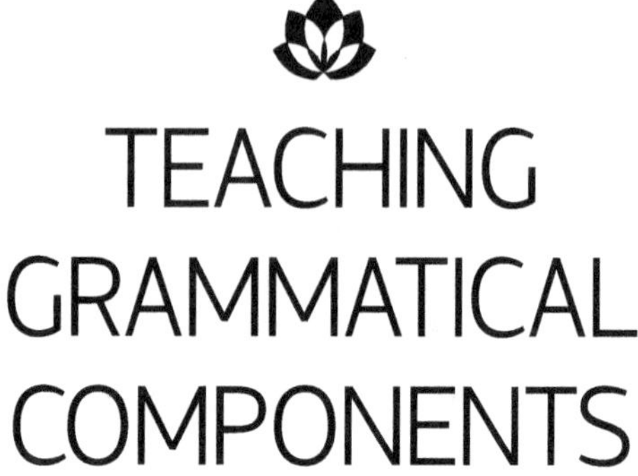

TEACHING GRAMMATICAL COMPONENTS

Grammar is the most essential part of any language. But it is always considered to be one of the toughest and less interesting components to be taught and learnt. But this component can be made interesting if the teacher can interact with students, make them come out with the aspects they already know and then explain them in detail. It is always better to induce games and fun activities in some form or other to ensure full participation of the students. The following are few games that can be used while teaching various components of grammar.

1. **Word scrappers:** In this game one student would begin giving a word that is a noun. The next student would add an article; the next would add an adjective and so on. Once all the components of Parts of Speech are induced, the last student would be asked to give it as a full sentence. Since the students themselves add words to words, they would make sure they add meaningful words to make a complete sentence. This would not only make them familiar with the Parts of Speech but also help them frame larger sentences. Example: Apple - The apple – The big apple – The big apple was eaten – The big apple was eaten slowly- The big apple was eaten slowly by me – The big apple was eaten slowly by me and my friend – Oh! The big apple was eaten slowly by me and my friend.

2. **Story with actions:** In this method the students could be asked to choose a short story of their choice. Each student can be given one component which he or she will have to just enact wherever it occurs instead of telling it out. Example: If a student is given prepositions, while narrating the story, whenever a preposition occurs, he or she has to enact that particular

preposition so that other students would try and identify the same. This method would help the student who enacts to identify prepositions in the story and will help the other students to learn various prepositions. Whenever a student misses out a preposition the teacher could help out with the same.

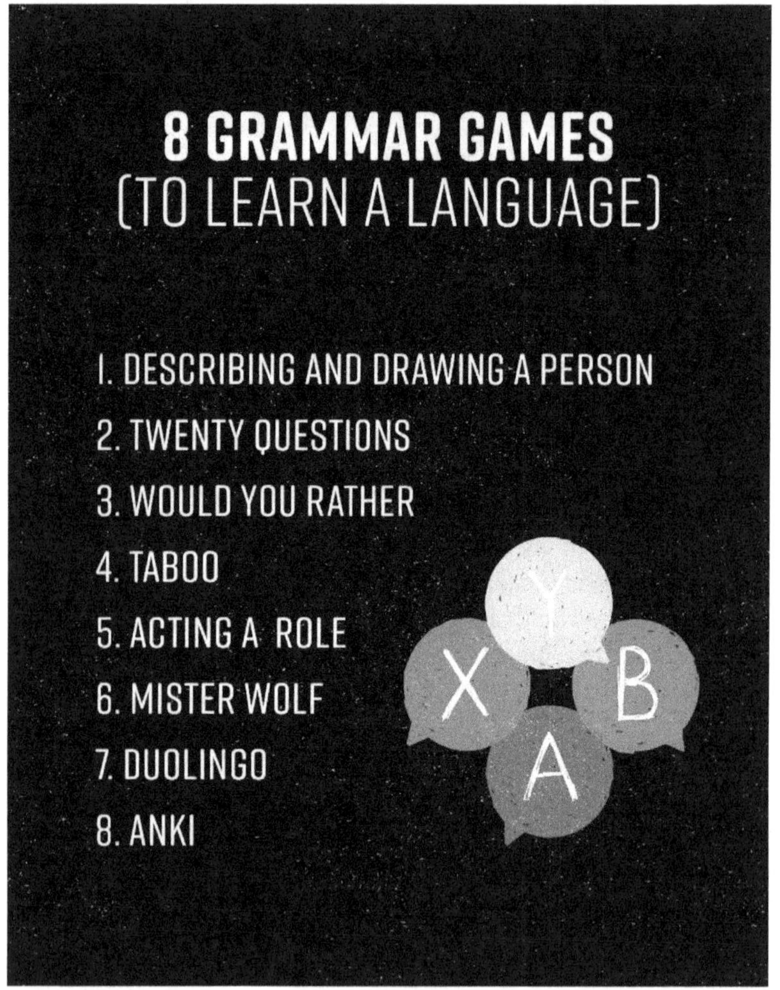

FEW MORE TO TRY

CHAPTER FOURTEEN

IMPORTANCE OF LEARNING ENGLISH

English is the need of the hour and there is an urge to learn the language thoroughly in every individual. When the schools and colleges fail to help the learners with learning the language properly, only then they start looking out for extra help. Even if teachers do their best to put all their expertise in teaching, improper interaction and failure to involve all the students in the classroom activities would result in failures. Since every student today has easy access to computers and the web they easily acquire the basics of English and grammar through web sources. Hence teachers must understand that what students really need; whether the basics or explanations, and then plan their teaching methods accordingly. In all the scenarios play-way method of teaching languages will definitely prove fruitful. Irrespective or the age group, every individual today looks for an atmosphere where learning would be pleasant, where teachers would respect their level of understanding and provide them with ample knowledge according to their level of understanding. The students expect innovations and creativity from teachers in all possible ways. Hence it is inimitable that the exuberance in teaching and learning languages lies in the creative and innovative applications of the teachers.

THE THREE LEVELS OF COMMUNICATION SKILLS

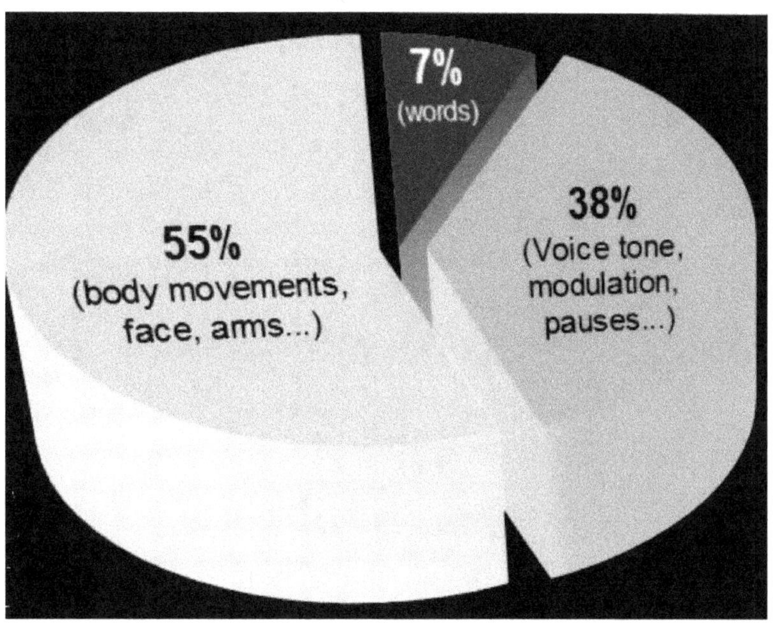

Here are a few interesting facts to understand how we communicate.

- *7% of what we communicate is based on vocabulary*

- *38% of what we communicate is based on voice inflexions*
- *55% of what we communicate is based on non-verbal behaviour*

So, the more we try to incorporate positive non-verbal techniques while communicating, the better the response. This holds very true for teachers. Since they deal with a variety of students batch after batch, it is good to keep ourselves updated to receive a positive response.

CHAPTER SIXTEEN

FUN ICEBREAKER ACTIVITIES

Activity 1: INTRODUCTION BINGO

- Participants are each given a special "Introduction Bingo" card and instructed to find other participants who meet the criteria of each block on the card.
- 30 minutes can be given
- Instruct participants that they should write the name of the person who meets the criteria of each block. The winner will be asked later whose name is in each block.

- Tell participants that when the first person has BINGO (a completed row either vertically, horizontally, or diagonally), he or she should shout out "BINGO."
- Once someone has BINGO, have participants return to their seats.
- Ask the Bingo winner to share the names of the participants in each block of their completed Bingo card.
- Ask those individuals whose names are on the card to briefly elaborate on their experiences that qualified him or her for their respective block.
- After each person on the winner's Bingo card has explained his or her experiences or interests, thank everyone for their participation and tell them that this activity will help the program go better because everyone knows each other a little better.

Introduction Bingo

Drives an SUV or a truck	Likes poetry	Asks for directions when driving	Plays a musical instrument	Does own ironing
Owns an Apple computer	Has visited Canada	Collects something as a hobby	Reads more than one daily newspaper	Has ridden on a passenger train
Speaks a foreign language	Watches TV game shows	FREE SPACE	Eats out at least twice a week	Beatles fan
Loves hockey	Visited Washington, D.C. as a child	Has met a famous person	Recently bought a new car	Goes to the movies at least once a month
Has been to the opera	Likes country music	Rides a bicycle to work	Owns a big screen TV	Plays golf

Activity 1 Sheet

Activity 2: FOLLOWING DIRECTIONS

- Participants are provided with a worksheet and told to follow very specific instructions to complete the assigned tasks from the facilitator.
- Distribute the handout to each participant. Tell them to do exactly as you instruct them to do to test their listening skills and

ability to follow directions.

Following Directions Worksheet

<table>
<tr><td>1.

I</td><td>2.

— — — — — —</td></tr>
<tr><td>3.

MB BB PB</td><td>4.

OODRWWTS</td></tr>
</table>

Activity 2 Handout 1

- Tell participants that in quadrant one they should place a dot on the litter "I."
- In quadrant two, tell participants to print the word XEROX in the spaces provided.
- In quadrant three, explain that PB stands for Papa Bull, MB stands for Mamma Bull, and BB stands for Baby Bull. Ask participants which is the odd one.
- In quadrant four, ask participants to spell two words using the letters shown.

- After participants have completed the worksheet, drawout the actual answers and which shows the way the worksheet should have been completed if one followed the directions exactly.

Following Directions Worksheet: Answers

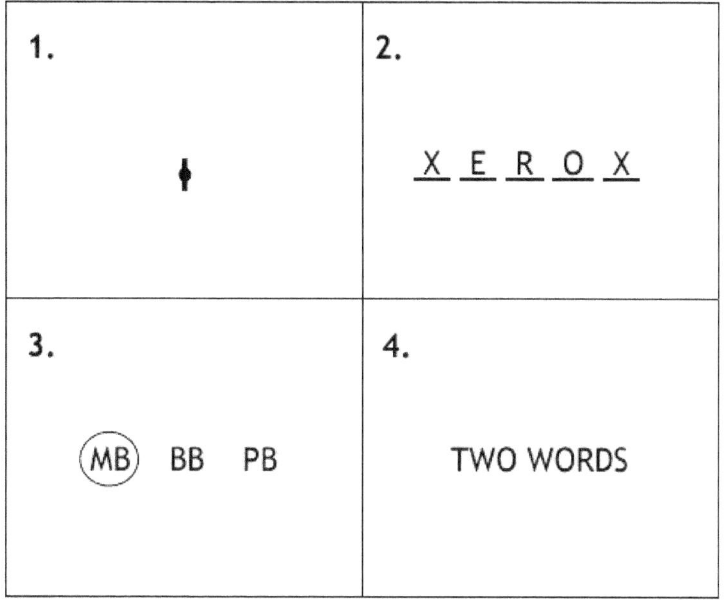

Activity 2 Answers

- Remind participants that the instructions told them to place a dot on the letter "I" and to write XEROX in the spaces provided in quadrant two. Explain that in quadrant three there is no such thing as a Mamma Bull—she would be a cow! Finally, in quadrant four, tell the participants all they had to do was spell two words using the letters that were simply jumbled up.

Activity 3: COUNT THE NUMBER OF "S"

- Participants are to be presented with a sentence and asked to identify how many times the letter S appears.
- Ask them to reveal the number they have arrived at. The answers might vary from person to person.
- Explain that one of the reasons that it may be so difficult to identify all of the letter Ss in the sentence is that S has a number of different sounds to it depending on its context. Often the softer sounds can easily become camouflaged or hidden within words.
- Finally show them the places where the "S"s appear.

Super Sunday

Super Sunday often results in many surprises as fans watch with great anticipation to see if their favorite team wins the ultimate prize in professional football each season.

Activity 3 Handout

Super Sunday

Super Sunday often results in many surprises as fans watch with great anticipation to see if their favorite team wins the ultimate prize in professional football each season.

Activity 3 Answers

COMMUNICATION SHUTDOWNS

Several times, in official scenarios, we might notice our colleagues abruptly stop their conversation. When we ask them if they were about to add more points or if they had something to say, they simply would evade the question and move over. Have you wondered why? This is because they might have been offended because of any of the phrases that are called "Communication Shutdowns". They might not be directly offensive, but they are highly unprofessional, and might not be received too well. Given below are a few communication shutdown phrases.

Communications Shutdowns

1. Don't be ridiculous.
2. It'll cost too much.
3. That's not my responsibility.
4. We don't have time.
5. We've never done that before.
6. That's not the way we do things around here.
7. If it ain't broke, don't fix it.
8. We're not ready for that.
9. You can't teach an old dog new tricks.
10. It will never sell.
11. We will become the laughing stock of the entire company.
12. We tried that before and it didn't work.
13. It simply can't be done.
14. It's too radical of a change.
15. That will make our current equipment obsolete.
16. It's not really our problem.
17. Let's get back to reality.
18. Let's form a committee to decide.
19. I need to go over the numbers again.
20. It's not in our budget.
21. We have done alright without it all this time.
22. It won't work here.
23. Okay, but if it doesn't work, you're the one who's going to get the blame.
24. I don't personally agree, but if you insist.
25. Are you crazy?

Examples

CLASSROOM RULES

The classroom should have the decorum to maintain. Set clear expectations and put a set of rules in place for structured functioning. This should be a simple and easily understandable set of instructions, which your student starts following from the first day.

When setting out these rules on the first day, make sure they are verbal and have clear, precise written instructions. Put the written instructions in a prominent place in the classroom so it is visible at all times. If and when a student steps out of line, refer to these rules and ensure the entire class understands what is acceptable and what is not.

Without set rules in place, there would be no discipline in class, and students will not understand your expectations correctly. There will be a lot of wasted time telling your students off, instead of focusing on either teaching or learning English as a second language.

CHAPTER NINETEEN

USE TECHNOLOGY

Technology has evolved at a fast pace, and still, new technology is being introduced daily. We are learning, and our students can be more tech-savvy than us! Teaching methods are continually evolving too, and as a teacher, you should keep abreast too! It is a digital age today, and with smart boards and learning apps, the use of technology is vital in an active learning process.

There is a lot of teaching and training material available on the internet. To connect with your tech-savvy student as well as make your class enjoyable, you can use short clips, language apps, and music in your classroom.

Rather than using printed materials, you could also send worksheets, questionnaires, presentations, etc. to their phones or emails. This will allow keeping things in one place even without paper, and students can also revisit or prepare for class in advance.

Just bear in mind that not all students or countries have the same level of devices or technology. So it's essential to use these methods after establishing facts.

Social Media

Social Media is also a great way to teach English as a second language. Many of your students will be well-versed in Social media. It will prove to be a treasure trove or you to teach colloquial phrases and commonly used words. Besides, it provides an excellent chance for students to learn word usage and practice.

Gustiar Fathqi , Institut Teknologi Sepuluh Nopember (ITS), Surabaya, Indonesia in a paper titled "Learning English Through Social Media" has written that social media provides several opportunities for learning languages. It does not restrict people based on their background, or age, or gender.

CHAPTER TWENTY

PROBLEMS FACED BY INDIAN STUDENTS WHILE LEARNING ENGLISH AS A SECOND LANGUAGE

India is known for its variety of cultures and religions. With this comes different languages as well. Though Hindi is recorded as the National Language of India, one cannot deny that ever since the British ruled and left us an independent nation, English slowly crept into the culture of the nation. Today English is actually the connecting language. This being said, it is to be agreed that the variety of languages causes moderate to severe difficulty in learning English. There is always a visible influence of one's mother tongue, however fluent the speaker might be. Of all Indians, a popular study states that Tamil-speaking people have the best neutral accent, much closer to a native English speaker. This is because most of the phonetics are similar in both languages and there is very less deviations.

What are the factors that affect a person learning English as a second language?

Pronunciation

Native languages influence pronunciations of English syllables/words, e.g. people who speak north Indian languages usually pronounce the word 'here' as 'hare/hair', and people from the east often interchange the /s/ and /sh/ sounds while speaking English. The speakers from southern states roll their /l/ sounds quite harshly. Most Indians stress on the last syllable while speaking English.

Exposure to English

Indian learners who are exposed to English from kindergarten and at home learn and use the language better than those who start learning English from primary school and above. Since English is widely spoken across the globe, most young urban parents make it a point to expose their children to English early on. Education in native languages remains quite popular in non-urban locales; therefore, we've observed that much of the rural populace have a marked influence of their first language while using English.

Differences in Language Structure

Some differences between English and Indian languages that affect learning - the word order of sentences in Indian languages as well as the rules of grammar are quite different from English. Indian languages have a phonetic base, unlike English. This affects how they understand spelling and English phonetics.

Consonant sounds in Indian languages are quite harsh, compared to the softer English counterparts. There are intonational differences from speakers from different regions. Therefore, understanding tonality and applying it while speaking in English can also be tricky, e.g. detecting sarcasm is challenging for most Indians.

Translation Approach

The most common error made by Indian learners is a direct translation of sentences/phrases from their first language to English. The reason behind this is the way the language has been taught to the learner. In the initial phase of learning, basic words are taught through pictorial representations or translation. While this is necessary to a certain degree, English teachers continue to use translation in higher classes as well. This prevents students from understanding the nuances of the language. This, in turn, affects their thought groups and sentence construction. Ultimately this affects the fluency of speech, as they're unable to use English to express themselves efficiently.

Vocabulary Challenge

Synonyms and antonyms are understood quite well as concepts; however, the use of synonymous words in degrees can be difficult. Indians often use double superlatives, or repeat words, to emphasize a point, e.g. 'biggest', 'it's in different-different rooms'; this is a cultural influence rather than a linguistic one.

While teaching English to Indian learners, it's important to explain cultural contexts including idioms and slang (American, British, Australian), so that they understand how the language is used. It is also advised to cover politically correct terms in English, as most non-urban Indian learners are not exposed to them.

Due to the popularity of American television series, most Indians can understand the American accent quite well. However, they may often struggle to understand British or Australian accents.

CHAPTER TWENTY-ONE

TEACHING TECHNIQUES

Teaching is an interesting task, but also a challenging one. It is more challenging when a teacher is bestowed with the task of teaching English to non-natives. The following are popular methods that have been proved effective in teaching English as a second language to non-native learners.

Communicative language teaching

Communicative language teaching (CLT) emphasizes interaction as both the means and the ultimate goal of learning a language. Despite a number of criticisms, it continues to be popular, particularly in Japan, Taiwan, and Europe. In India, CBSE (Central Board of Secondary Education) has adopted this approach in its affiliated schools.

The task-based language learning approach to CLT has gained ground in recent years. Proponents believe CLT is important for developing and improving speaking, writing, listening, and reading skills and that it prevents students from merely listening passively to the teacher without actually interacting. Dogme is a similar communicative approach that encourages teaching without published textbooks, instead focusing on conversational communication among the learners and the teacher.

Blended learning

Blended learning is a combination of multimedia elements (also known as computer-assisted language learning), achieved through a virtual learning environment (VLE) with classroom instruction, a teacher, and peers. Blended learning utilizes technology to provide massive amounts of comprehensible input to its learners through video and other types of multimedia without a teacher present.

Online classroom

Advances in technology have made it possible to get a TEFL qualification online. Students can enroll in online classes that are accredited by organizations such as the British Council or Cambridge ESOL. There is no single overarching accreditation body for TEFL; however, private for-profit companies have been known to invent accreditation affiliates and use them to cheat the customer.

Study materials are divided into modules that students are tested on. Support is handled by tutors, who can be reached via email. After successfully finishing the last module, the student is granted a certificate that comes in digital form or can be shipped to the student's address. Getting such a certificate can be beneficial as many employers require a TEFL certificate.

CHAPTER TWENTY-TWO

LANGUAGE PEDAGOGY

Pedagogy means the process of education. This involves both teaching and learning. Language pedagogy is concerned with theories and practical of learning languages; especially English.

There are several methods in language pedagogy but they can be classified into three: structural, functional, and interactive.

1. The structural view treats language as a system of structurally related elements to code meaning (e.g. grammar).
2. The functional view sees language as a vehicle to express or accomplish certain functions, (e.g. making a request, giving information or asking for information).
3. The interactive view sees language as a vehicle for the creation and maintenance of social relations, focusing on patterns of moves, acts, negotiation and interaction found in conversational exchanges. This view has been fairly dominant since the 1980s.

CHAPTER TWENTY-THREE

PROMOTING LEARNER AUTONOMY

Learner autonomy encourages the learner to be self-governing and self-motivated and thus makes language learning more successful and optimistic. Holec, sees "Autonomous Learning is a double process, it entails learning the foreign language and learning how to learn". Students have more responsibility than teachers in learning process. Teacher should adapt a method of teaching which has a good reach among the students. Teacher should always be friendly with the students.

They should not impose their ideas on the students. They should always be approachable and they should build a good rapport with the students. Effective activities must be conducted and it is the responsibility of the teacher to make the students participate enthusiastically. Competitions to improve the language learning can be conducted by dividing the students into groups and by naming each group to make the students take part actively. Small prizes can be given to the team which won thereby, creating an interest among the students. Teachers should give individual attention especially to the slow learners. Learners' goals and talents should be identified and they should be channelized properly. Teachers should encourage and motivate the learners to bring out their talents. The teachers be supposed to give them confidence that they can achieve their goals. Students always expect a pat on their back and teachers should be a good motivator and a facilitator.

Besides, the learners should also be interactive and cooperative with the teachers to succeed in their endeavors.

FOR LANGUGAE LEARNERS

TIPS TO IMPROVE SPOKEN COMMUNICATION

(Suggested by WikiHow)

1. Attend an English class or discussion group.

A great way to incorporate some English conversation into your routine is to join a class of discussion group.

Attending an English class is a great way to focus on some of the more formal aspects of speaking English. A class will teach you the grammatically correct way of speaking -- which includes proper sentence structure and verb conjugation and will generally provide a very structured approach to language learning.

Attending a discussion group is a more informal and relaxed way of learning English, where the emphasis is more on communication and relationship building than on speaking "correct" English. Speaking English in this setting can help you to become more comfortable with speaking in front of other people.

Both of these language-learning settings have their pros and cons, so it's best to do both if you can!

2. Speak a little English every day.

The absolute best way to learn any new language is just to speak it. It doesn't matter if you only know five English words or if you're practically fluent -- speaking English with another person is the fastest, most effective method of improving.

Don't wait until you "feel more comfortable" speaking in English -- you probably won't reach that level for a long time, so push yourself outside of your comfort zone and start speaking English today. You'll be amazed at how quickly your language skills improve.

Find a native English speaker who is willing to spend some time speaking English with you -- you may be able to offer them a language exchange, where they spend 30 minutes speaking English with you and you spend 30 minutes speaking your native language with them.

If you live in an English-speaking country, you can practice by starting simple conversations with the people you meet, whether it's saying "hello" to a shopkeeper or asking a stranger for directions.

3. Work on your pronunciation.

Even if you have an acceptable grasp of the English language, with good grammar and an extensive vocabulary, native English speakers may find you very difficult to understand if you don't work on your pronunciation.

Correct, clear pronunciation is essential if you really want to improve your level of English. Listen closely to how native English speakers pronounce certain words and sounds and do your best to copy them.

Pay particular attention to any sounds that you are unfamiliar with or that do not exist in your native tongue. For example, some people have difficulty pronouncing the "r" sound, as it does not exist in their native language, while other people have difficulty with certain consonant clusters, such as the "th" sound.

Be aware that the pronunciation of certain English words varies greatly depending on the part of the world it's spoken in. For example, American English is very different from British English. If you intend to travel to or live in an English-speaking country, this is something you should take into account when learning how to pronounce certain words.

4. Expand your vocabulary and use idiomatic phrases.

The wider your vocabulary and the more English phrases you learn, the easier speaking English will become.

Again, spending time with native English speakers will help you to pick up on common vocabulary and phrases in a natural way. Although reading, watching English TV and listening to the news is also beneficial.

Once you have learned a new word or phrase, you should make an effort to use it in a sentence -- this is the best way to commit it to memory.

Another easy way to commit new words to memory is to make labels for everyday household items and stick them around your house or apartment. Then every time you use the kettle or look in the mirror, you will see the English word for these items staring back at you.

You should also start a notebook of idiomatic phrases that English speakers use all the time. Some examples include "it's raining cats and dogs" (raining heavily), to be on "cloud nine" (to be very happy) or saying something is a "piece of cake" (when something is very easy). Sprinkling these kinds of phrases into your conversation will bring your level of English up several notches.

5. Carry a dictionary.

Carrying an English dictionary with you at all times (whether it's an actual book or a phone app) can be very useful.

Having a dictionary means that you will never be stuck for a word. It can save you a lot of embarrassment if you're having a conversation with an English-speaker and forget a word in the middle of the sentence -- all you have to do is take a second to look it up!

Aside from saving you awkwardness, looking up the word you need then immediately using it in a sentence will actually help you to commit the new vocabulary to memory.

It is also helpful to have a dictionary to peruse throughout the day during private moments, like when you're sitting on the train, waiting to cross the street or just having a cup of coffee. You could learn an extra 20 to 30 English words per day using this technique!

As a beginner, you should start with an English dictionary that provides definitions in your native language. However, once your language skills improve, you should switch to using an English-English dictionary, which provides English definitions for English words.

If you are just going to a store and you think it would be impossible to bring a giant dictionary, you can always just bring your phone/tablet, which has a translator!

References

1. "English as a Second or Foreign Language." Wikipedia, Wikimedia Foundation, 13 Oct. 2022, https://en.wikipedia.org/wiki/English_as_a_second_or_foreign_language.
2. Garber, Peter R. 50 Communications Activities, Icebreakers, and Exercises. HRD Press, 2008.
3. "How to Learn English: 15 Steps (with Pictures)." WikiHow, WikiHow, https://www.wikihow.com/Learn-English.
4. Jackie. "Sentence Building Games and Activities: ESL Sentence Structure." ESL Activities, 16 Aug. 2022, https://www.eslactivity.org/sentences-structure-games/.
5. Marlina, Roby. The Pedagogy of English as an International Language: Perspectives from Scholars, Teachers, and Students. Springer, 2014.
6. Richards, Jack C., and Theodore S. Rodgers. Approaches and Methods in Language Teaching. Cambridge University Press, 2012.
7. "Teaching English as a Second or Foreign Language." Wikipedia, Wikimedia Foundation, 24 Oct. 2022,
8. "English Language Learning Clubs: A Novel Approach to Improving EFL Students' Verbal Communication Skills." International Journal on Studies in English Language and Literature, vol. 9, no. 7, 2021, https://doi.org/10.20431/2347-3134.0907001.